**Grade 1**

# Subtraction Activities

Written by **Eliza Berkowitz**

Illustrations by **Maru Jara**

FlashKids

An imprint of Sterling Children's Books

# This book belongs to

_____

FLASH KIDS, STERLING, and the distinctive Sterling logo are registered trademarks of
Sterling Publishing Co., Inc.

Published by Sterling Publishing Co., Inc.
387 Park Avenue South, New York, NY 10016
Text and illustrations © 2006 by Flash Kids
Distributed in Canada by Sterling Publishing
c/o Canadian Manda Group, 165 Dufferin Street
Toronto, Ontario, Canada M6K 3H6
Distributed in the United Kingdom by GMC Distribution Services
Castle Place, 166 High Street, Lewes, East Sussex, England BN7 1XU
Distributed in Australia by Capricorn Link (Australia) Pty. Ltd.
P.O. Box 704, Windsor, NSW 2756, Australia

Sterling ISBN 978-1-4114-3457-8

Manufactured in China

Lot #:
2  4  6  8  10  9  7  5  3
10/11

For information about custom editions, special sales, premium and
corporate purchases, please contact Sterling Special Sales
Department at 800-805-5489 or specialsales@sterlingpublishing.com.

Cover design and production by Mada Design, Inc.

# Dear Parent,

To reinforce what your child learns in the classroom, it is helpful to provide your child with activities he or she can do at home. This book will help your child learn the basics of subtraction by providing fun activities your child will enjoy. To get the most from this book, follow these simple steps:

- Find a comfortable place where you and your child can work quietly together.
- Encourage your child to go at his or her own pace.
- Help your child work out the problems.
- Offer lots of praise and support.
- Let your child reward his or her work with the included stickers.
- Most of all, remember that learning should be fun! Take time to look at the pictures, laugh at the funny characters, and enjoy this special time spent together.

# upcakes for Everyone!

tract the numbers. Write the answers in the cupcakes.

1.
$$3$$
$$-0$$

3

2.
$$5$$
$$-2$$

3

3.
$$4$$
$$-3$$

1

4.
$$2$$
$$-2$$

0

5.
$$3$$
$$-0$$

3

6.
$$2$$
$$-1$$

1

7.
$$3$$
$$-2$$

1

8.
$$2$$
$$-0$$

2

# Tasty T

Subtract the numbers. Write f... ...ollipops.

1.
$$\begin{array}{r} 2 \\ -\ 2 \\ \hline \end{array}$$
0

2.
$$\begin{array}{r} 6 \\ -\ 3 \\ \hline \end{array}$$
3

3.
$$\begin{array}{r} 3 \\ -\ 2 \\ \hline \end{array}$$
1

4.
$$\begin{array}{r} 1 \\ -\ 0 \\ \hline \end{array}$$
1

5.
$$\begin{array}{r} 3 \\ -\ 1 \\ \hline \end{array}$$
2

6.
$$\begin{array}{r} 4 \\ -\ 2 \\ \hline \end{array}$$
2

7.
$$\begin{array}{r} 2 \\ -\ 1 \\ \hline \end{array}$$
1

8.
$$\begin{array}{r} 4 \\ -\ 3 \\ \hline \end{array}$$
1

# So Many Sweets

Subtract the sweets. Write the answers on the lines.

1.

 —  = $2$

2.

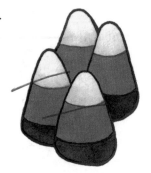  = $3$

3.

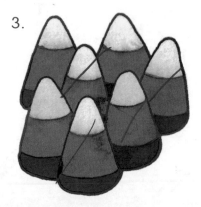 —  = $3$

# More Marshmallows

Subtract the marshmallows. Write the answers on the lines.

1. 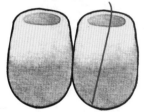 — = _1_

2. 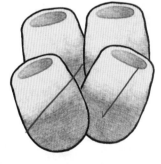 —  = _2_

3. 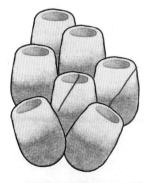 —  = _5_

# Cookie Club

Subtract the numbers.

1.
$$\begin{array}{r} 7 \\ -\,3 \\ \hline 4 \end{array}$$

2.
$$\begin{array}{r} 6 \\ -\,2 \\ \hline 4 \end{array}$$

3.
$$\begin{array}{r} 4 \\ -\,1 \\ \hline 3 \end{array}$$

4.
$$\begin{array}{r} 3 \\ -\,2 \\ \hline 1 \end{array}$$

5.
$$\begin{array}{r} 4 \\ -\,4 \\ \hline 0 \end{array}$$

6.
$$\begin{array}{r} 3 \\ -\,1 \\ \hline 2 \end{array}$$

7.
$$\begin{array}{r} 5 \\ -\,3 \\ \hline 2 \end{array}$$

8.
$$\begin{array}{r} 2 \\ -\,2 \\ \hline 0 \end{array}$$

# Fun Fruits

Subtract the numbers.

1.
$$\begin{array}{r} 6 \\ -1 \\ \hline 5 \end{array}$$

2.
$$\begin{array}{r} 4 \\ -3 \\ \hline 1 \end{array}$$

3.
$$\begin{array}{r} 5 \\ -2 \\ \hline 3 \end{array}$$

4.
$$\begin{array}{r} 7 \\ -3 \\ \hline 4 \end{array}$$

5.
$$\begin{array}{r} 4 \\ -1 \\ \hline 3 \end{array}$$

6.
$$\begin{array}{r} 5 \\ -4 \\ \hline 1 \end{array}$$

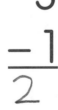

7.
$$\begin{array}{r} 3 \\ -1 \\ \hline 2 \end{array}$$

8.
$$\begin{array}{r} 4 \\ -0 \\ \hline 4 \end{array}$$

9

# A Terrific Treat!

Subtract the numbers.

Color the areas that have the number 2 for the answer.

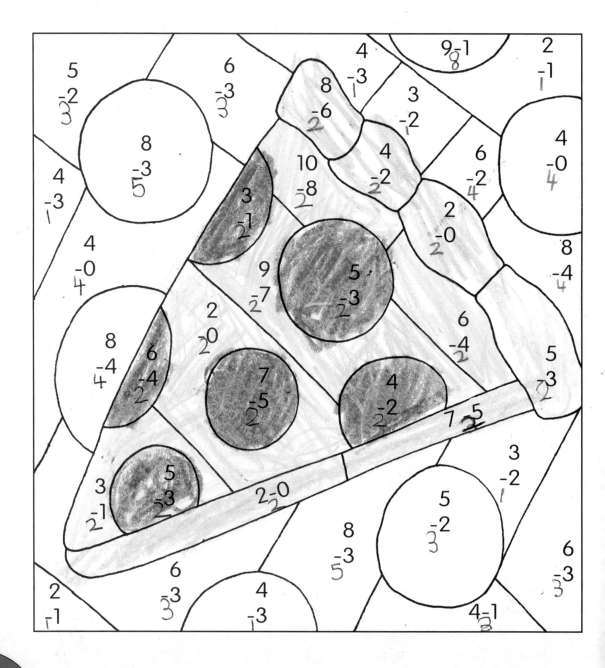

# Popping Popcorn

Subtract the popcorn. Write the answers on t

1.  $-$  $=$ 0.

2.  $-$  $=$ 2

3.  $-$  $=$ 2

# Time for Cake!

Subtract the numbers. Write the answers on the pieces of cake.

1. $$3 - 2 = 1$$

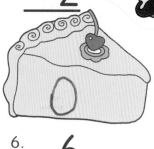

2. $$5 - 1 = 4$$

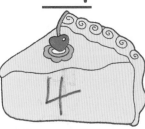

3. $$2 - 2 = 0$$

4. $$3 - 1 = 2$$

5. $$4 - 3 = 1$$

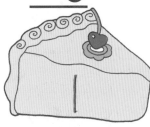

6. $$6 - 0 = 6$$

7. $$3 - 1 = 2$$

8. $$5 - 0 = 5$$

# Eat Your Veggies

Subtract the numbers.
Write the answers on the vegetables.

1.
$$5$$
$$-1$$

4

2.
$$3$$
$$-1$$

2

3.
$$4$$
$$-3$$

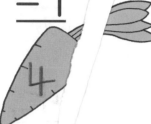
1

4.
$$-1$$

5

5.
$$5$$
$$-2$$

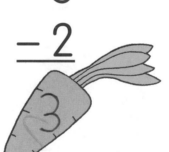
3

6.
$$4$$
$$-0$$

4

7.
$$4$$
$$-2$$

2

8.
$$5$$
$$-4$$

1

# Happy Hamburgers

Subtract the numbers.

1.
$$\begin{array}{r} 5 \\ -\ 5 \\ \hline 0 \end{array}$$

2.
$$\begin{array}{r} 4 \\ -\ 1 \\ \hline 3 \end{array}$$

3.
$$\begin{array}{r} 3 \\ -\ 2 \\ \hline 1 \end{array}$$

4.
$$\begin{array}{r} 6 \\ -\ 4 \\ \hline 2 \end{array}$$

5.
$$\begin{array}{r} 4 \\ -\ 2 \\ \hline 2 \end{array}$$

6.
$$\begin{array}{r} 7 \\ -\ 1 \\ \hline 6 \end{array}$$

7.
$$\begin{array}{r} 6 \\ -\ 2 \\ \hline 4 \end{array}$$

8.
$$\begin{array}{r} 5 \\ -\ 2 \\ \hline 3 \end{array}$$

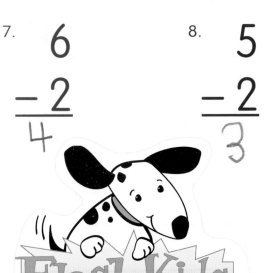

# Bagels for Breakfast

Subtract the numbers. Write the answers on the bagels.

1.
$$4 - 2 = 2$$

2.
$$2 - 2 = 0$$

3.
$$3 - 0 = 3$$

4.
$$5 - 4 = 1$$

5.
$$6 - 5 = 1$$

6.
$$4 - 1 = 3$$

7.
$$5 - 5 = 0$$

8.
$$6 - 3 = 3$$

# A Sweet Treat!

Subtract the numbers.

Color the areas that have the number 3 for the answer.

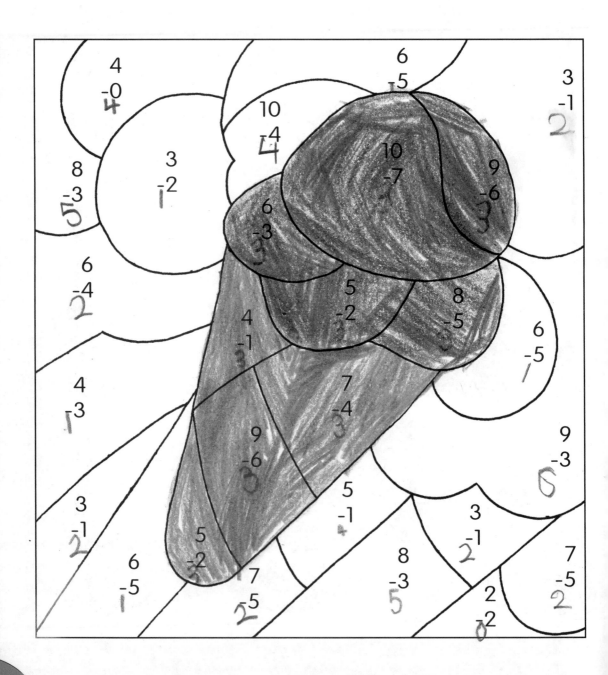

# Do You Like Candy Bars?

Subtract the candy bars.

Write the answers on the lines.

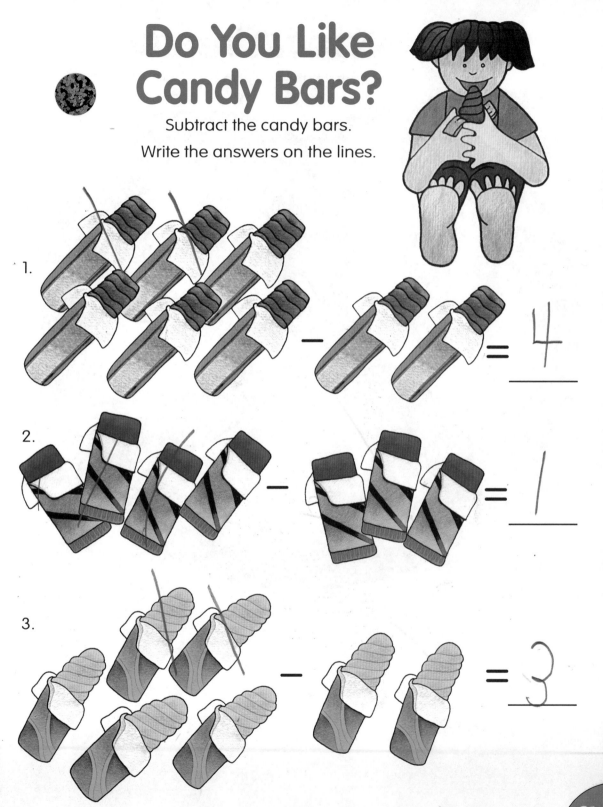

1. $-$ $=$ 4

2. $-$ $=$ 1

3. $-$ $=$ 3

# A Perfect Pretzel

Subtract the numbers.

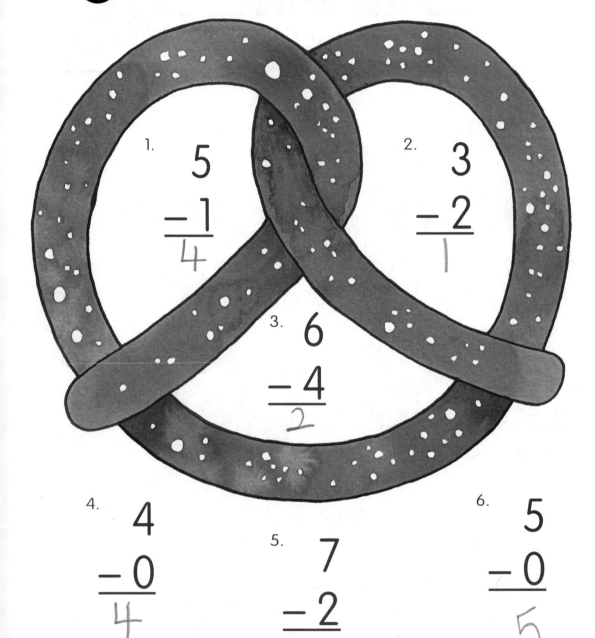

1.
$$\begin{array}{r} 5 \\ -1 \\ \hline 4 \end{array}$$

2.
$$\begin{array}{r} 3 \\ -2 \\ \hline 1 \end{array}$$

3.
$$\begin{array}{r} 6 \\ -4 \\ \hline 2 \end{array}$$

4.
$$\begin{array}{r} 4 \\ -0 \\ \hline 4 \end{array}$$

5.
$$\begin{array}{r} 7 \\ -2 \\ \hline 5 \end{array}$$

6.
$$\begin{array}{r} 5 \\ -0 \\ \hline 5 \end{array}$$

# How Many Cupcakes?

Write the answers on the lines.

1. Megan had 6 cupcakes.
   She gave 2 to her friends.
   How many cupcakes did
   Megan have left? 4

2. John had 3 cupcakes.
   He gave 2 to his friends.
   How many cupcakes did
   John have left? 1

3. Grace had 5 cupcakes.
   She gave 3 to her friends.
   How many cupcakes did
   Grace have left? 2

# A Pizza Party

Subtract the pieces of pizza.

Write the answers on the lines.

  —    = 2 ___

2.   —    = 3 ___

3.   —    = 1 ___

# Chewy Cookies

Subtract the cookies. Write the answers on the lines.

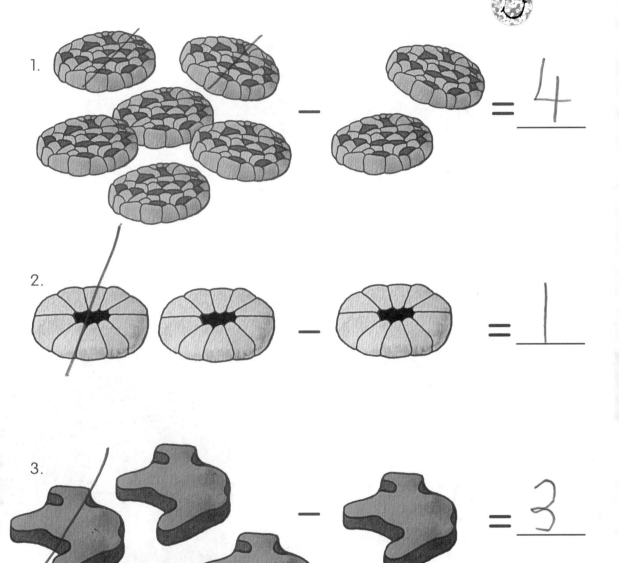

1. $-\ \ =\ 4$

2. $-\ \ =\ 1$

3. $-\ \ =\ 3$

# Great Grapes

Subtract the numbers.

1.
$$
\begin{array}{r}
6 \\
-\ 4 \\
\hline
2
\end{array}
$$

2.
$$
\begin{array}{r}
7 \\
-\ 2 \\
\hline
5
\end{array}
$$

3.
$$
\begin{array}{r}
5 \\
-\ 3 \\
\hline
2
\end{array}
$$

4.
$$
\begin{array}{r}
4 \\
-\ 0 \\
\hline
4
\end{array}
$$

5.
$$
\begin{array}{r}
8 \\
-\ 6 \\
\hline
2
\end{array}
$$

6.
$$
\begin{array}{r}
5 \\
-\ 1 \\
\hline
4
\end{array}
$$

7.
$$
\begin{array}{r}
7 \\
-\ 0 \\
\hline
7
\end{array}
$$

8.
$$
\begin{array}{r}
6 \\
-\ 5 \\
\hline
1
\end{array}
$$

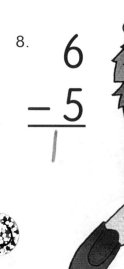

# Cool Candy

Subtract the numbers.

1.
$$\begin{array}{r} 5 \\ -\ 5 \\ \hline 0 \end{array}$$

2.
$$\begin{array}{r} 8 \\ -\ 4 \\ \hline 4 \end{array}$$

3.
$$\begin{array}{r} 7 \\ -\ 6 \\ \hline 1 \end{array}$$

4.
$$\begin{array}{r} 9 \\ -\ 5 \\ \hline 4 \end{array}$$

5.
$$\begin{array}{r} 5 \\ -\ 4 \\ \hline 1 \end{array}$$

6.
$$\begin{array}{r} 6 \\ -\ 6 \\ \hline 0 \end{array}$$

7.
$$\begin{array}{r} 9 \\ -\ 3 \\ \hline 6 \end{array}$$

8.
$$\begin{array}{r} 7 \\ -\ 5 \\ \hline 2 \end{array}$$

# Perfect Pies

Subtract the numbers.

1.
$$
\begin{array}{r}
6 \\
-5 \\
\hline 1
\end{array}
$$

2.
$$
\begin{array}{r}
8 \\
-2 \\
\hline 6
\end{array}
$$

3.
$$
\begin{array}{r}
4 \\
-4 \\
\hline 0
\end{array}
$$

4.
$$
\begin{array}{r}
9 \\
-5 \\
\hline 4
\end{array}
$$

5.
$$
\begin{array}{r}
8 \\
-7 \\
\hline 1
\end{array}
$$

6.
$$
\begin{array}{r}
6 \\
-3 \\
\hline 3
\end{array}
$$

7.
$$
\begin{array}{r}
8 \\
-3 \\
\hline 5
\end{array}
$$

8.
$$
\begin{array}{r}
9 \\
-4 \\
\hline 5
\end{array}
$$

# Excellent Eggs

Subtract the numbers.

1.
$$\begin{array}{r} 8 \\ -\ 8 \\ \hline 0 \end{array}$$

2.
$$\begin{array}{r} 5 \\ -\ 4 \\ \hline 1 \end{array}$$

3.
$$\begin{array}{r} 7 \\ -\ 2 \\ \hline 5 \end{array}$$

4.
$$\begin{array}{r} 8 \\ -\ 4 \\ \hline 4 \end{array}$$

5.
$$\begin{array}{r} 4 \\ -\ 3 \\ \hline 1 \end{array}$$

6.
$$\begin{array}{r} 9 \\ -\ 2 \\ \hline 7 \end{array}$$

7.
$$\begin{array}{r} 7 \\ -\ 5 \\ \hline 2 \end{array}$$

8.
$$\begin{array}{r} 5 \\ -\ 1 \\ \hline 4 \end{array}$$

# What's for Dinner?

Subtract the numbers.

Color the areas that have the number 4 for the answer.

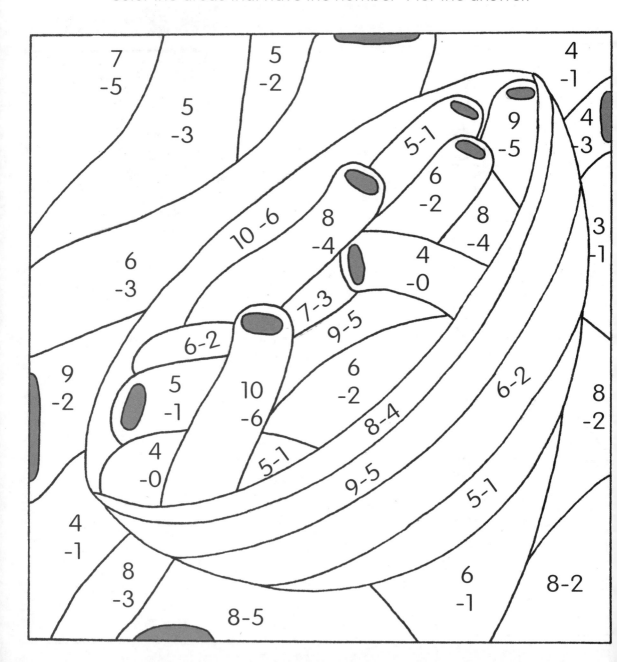

7
-5

5
-2

4
-1

5
-3

9
-5

4
-3

5-1

6
-2

8
-4

10 -6

8
-4

4
-0

3
-1

6
-3

7-3

9-5

6-2

5
-1

10
-6

6
-2

8-2

9
-2

8-4

6-2

4
-0

5-1

9-5

5-1

8

4
-1

8
-3

6
-1

8-2

8-5

# A Banana Boat

Subtract the numbers.

1.  $\begin{array}{r} 9 \\ -7 \\ \hline \end{array}$

2.  $\begin{array}{r} 5 \\ -5 \\ \hline \end{array}$

3.  $\begin{array}{r} 8 \\ -6 \\ \hline \end{array}$

4.  $\begin{array}{r} 4 \\ -3 \\ \hline \end{array}$

5.  $\begin{array}{r} 5 \\ -0 \\ \hline \end{array}$

6.  $\begin{array}{r} 6 \\ -4 \\ \hline \end{array}$

7.  $\begin{array}{r} 7 \\ -6 \\ \hline \end{array}$

8.  $\begin{array}{r} 8 \\ -2 \\ \hline \end{array}$

# A Potato Chip Party

Subtract the numbers.

1.
$$5 - 2$$

2.
$$6 - 5$$

3.
$$9 - 1$$

4.
$$2 - 2$$

5.
$$8 - 5$$

6.
$$7 - 4$$

7.
$$8 - 6$$

8.
$$9 - 2$$

# Wonderful Waffles

Subtract the numbers.

1. $\begin{array}{r} 5 \\ -3 \\ \hline \end{array}$

2. $\begin{array}{r} 8 \\ -4 \\ \hline \end{array}$

3. $\begin{array}{r} 7 \\ -2 \\ \hline \end{array}$

4. $\begin{array}{r} 6 \\ -3 \\ \hline \end{array}$

5. $\begin{array}{r} 9 \\ -4 \\ \hline \end{array}$

6. $\begin{array}{r} 4 \\ -3 \\ \hline \end{array}$

7. $\begin{array}{r} 7 \\ -5 \\ \hline \end{array}$

8. $\begin{array}{r} 8 \\ -7 \\ \hline \end{array}$

# Food Fight

Subtract the numbers. Write the answers on the apples.

Circle the fruit with the highest number.

1. 40
  − 30

2. 50
  − 10

3. 90
  − 60

4. 60
  − 40

5. 90
  − 20

6. 50
  − 40

7. 60
  − 20

8. 80
  − 50

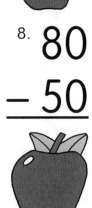

# Time for Dinner

Subtract the numbers. Write the answers on the plates.

Circle the plate with the highest number.

1. 
$$
\begin{array}{r}
70 \\
- 40 \\
\hline
\end{array}
$$
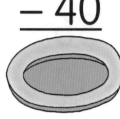

2. 
$$
\begin{array}{r}
90 \\
- 80 \\
\hline
\end{array}
$$
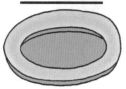

3. 
$$
\begin{array}{r}
50 \\
- 50 \\
\hline
\end{array}
$$
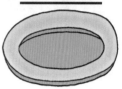

4. 
$$
\begin{array}{r}
60 \\
- 20 \\
\hline
\end{array}
$$

5. 
$$
\begin{array}{r}
70 \\
- 20 \\
\hline
\end{array}
$$

6. 
$$
\begin{array}{r}
80 \\
- 50 \\
\hline
\end{array}
$$

7. 
$$
\begin{array}{r}
50 \\
- 40 \\
\hline
\end{array}
$$

8. 
$$
\begin{array}{r}
70 \\
- 10 \\
\hline
\end{array}
$$
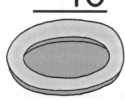

# We All Scream for Ice Cream!

Subtract the numbers.

1.
$$\begin{array}{r} 44 \\ -13 \\ \hline \end{array}$$

2.
$$\begin{array}{r} 56 \\ -12 \\ \hline \end{array}$$

3.
$$\begin{array}{r} 49 \\ -27 \\ \hline \end{array}$$

4.
$$\begin{array}{r} 53 \\ -12 \\ \hline \end{array}$$

5.
$$\begin{array}{r} 38 \\ -27 \\ \hline \end{array}$$

6.
$$\begin{array}{r} 45 \\ -22 \\ \hline \end{array}$$

7.
$$\begin{array}{r} 68 \\ -41 \\ \hline \end{array}$$

8.
$$\begin{array}{r} 43 \\ -21 \\ \hline \end{array}$$

# Peanut Butter and Jelly

Subtract the numbers.

1. 34
  − 13

2. 54
  − 21

3. 56
  − 32

4. 64
  − 24

5. 44
  − 20

6. 67
  − 34

7. 55
  − 32

8. 67
  − 43

# Silly Salad

Subtract the numbers. Write the answers on the lines.

Color the picture for some extra fun.

1. 22 – 12 = ____

2. 46 – 24 = ____

3. 32 – 22 = ____

4. 35 – 11 = ____

5. 42 – 31 = ____

6. 22 – 10 = ____

7. 56 – 24 = ____

8. 49 – 16 = ____

# Super Soup

Subtract the numbers. Write the answers on the lines.
Color the picture for some extra fun.

1. 44 – 22 = ___

2. 58 – 45 = ___

3. 22 – 2 = ___

4. 25 – 21 = ___

5. 57 – 11 = ___

6. 43 – 31 = ___

7. 39 – 18 = ___

8. 46 – 11 = ___

# A Super Snack!

Subtract the numbers.

Color the areas that have the number 5 for the answer.

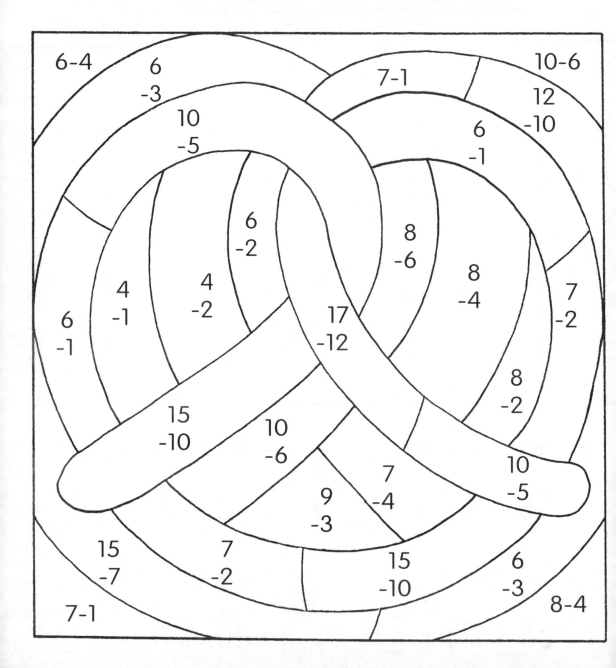

# A Sweet Guy!

Subtract the numbers.

1. 29
  − 17

2. 47
  − 36

3. 55
  − 23

4. 29
  − 18

5. 57
  − 32

6. 69
  − 24

7. 63
  − 13

8. 48
  − 26

# Crazy Cheese

Subtract the numbers.

1. 57
  − 24

2. 44
  − 23

3. 65
  − 12

4. 75
  − 35

5. 39
  − 12

6. 59
  − 37

7. 26
  − 15

8. 77
  − 34

# Great Big Glasses of Milk

Subtract the numbers. Write the answers in the glasses of milk.

1.
$$\begin{array}{r} 69 \\ -\ 22 \\ \hline \end{array}$$

2.
$$\begin{array}{r} 98 \\ -\ 26 \\ \hline \end{array}$$

3.
$$\begin{array}{r} 49 \\ -\ 45 \\ \hline \end{array}$$

4.
$$\begin{array}{r} 78 \\ -\ 48 \\ \hline \end{array}$$

5.
$$\begin{array}{r} 87 \\ -\ 24 \\ \hline \end{array}$$

6.
$$\begin{array}{r} 58 \\ -\ 23 \\ \hline \end{array}$$

7.
$$\begin{array}{r} 48 \\ -\ 27 \\ \hline \end{array}$$

8.
$$\begin{array}{r} 56 \\ -\ 12 \\ \hline \end{array}$$

# Yummy Pudding

Subtract the numbers.

1. 34
− 21

2. 69
− 36

3. 54
− 33

4. 67
− 34

5. 59
− 48

6. 67
− 21

7. 32
− 11

8. 45
− 30

# Cookies for Everyone!

Subtract the numbers.

1. 78
 − 54

2. 56
 − 45

3. 75
 − 30

4. 53
 − 21

5. 54
 − 33

6. 78
 − 47

7. 69
 − 56

8. 66
 − 45

# Slimy Spaghetti

Subtract the numbers.

1. $\begin{array}{r} 72 \\ -41 \\ \hline \end{array}$
2. $\begin{array}{r} 45 \\ -32 \\ \hline \end{array}$
3. $\begin{array}{r} 87 \\ -45 \\ \hline \end{array}$
4. $\begin{array}{r} 68 \\ -42 \\ \hline \end{array}$

5. $\begin{array}{r} 75 \\ -44 \\ \hline \end{array}$
6. $\begin{array}{r} 35 \\ -32 \\ \hline \end{array}$
7. $\begin{array}{r} 78 \\ -56 \\ \hline \end{array}$
8. $\begin{array}{r} 55 \\ -43 \\ \hline \end{array}$

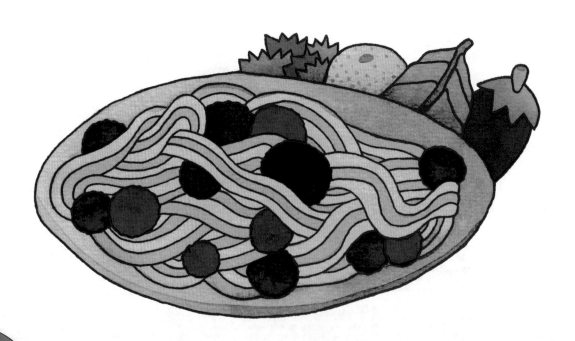

# Piles of Popcorn

Subtract the numbers.

1.
$$\begin{array}{r} 61 \\ -\ 40 \\ \hline \end{array}$$

2.
$$\begin{array}{r} 77 \\ -\ 52 \\ \hline \end{array}$$

3.
$$\begin{array}{r} 69 \\ -\ 33 \\ \hline \end{array}$$

4.
$$\begin{array}{r} 83 \\ -\ 21 \\ \hline \end{array}$$

5.
$$\begin{array}{r} 65 \\ -\ 35 \\ \hline \end{array}$$

6.
$$\begin{array}{r} 95 \\ -\ 43 \\ \hline \end{array}$$

7.
$$\begin{array}{r} 68 \\ -\ 54 \\ \hline \end{array}$$

8.
$$\begin{array}{r} 77 \\ -\ 43 \\ \hline \end{array}$$

# The Best Banana

Subtract the numbers.

1.  61
  − 20

2.  43
  − 12

3.  44
  − 10

4.  52
  − 12

5.  58
  − 56

6.  83
  − 22

7.  51
  − 10

8.  49
  − 12

# Plate of Pizza

Fill in the blanks.

Tyler and his friends are having a pizza party.

1. If they had 44 pieces of pizza and
   they ate 21, how many are left? _____

2. If they had 67 pieces of pizza and
   they ate 43, how many are left? _____

3. If they had 83 pieces of pizza and
   they ate 32, how many are left? _____

# Fun and Fruity!

Subtract the numbers.

Color the areas that have the number 6 for the answer.

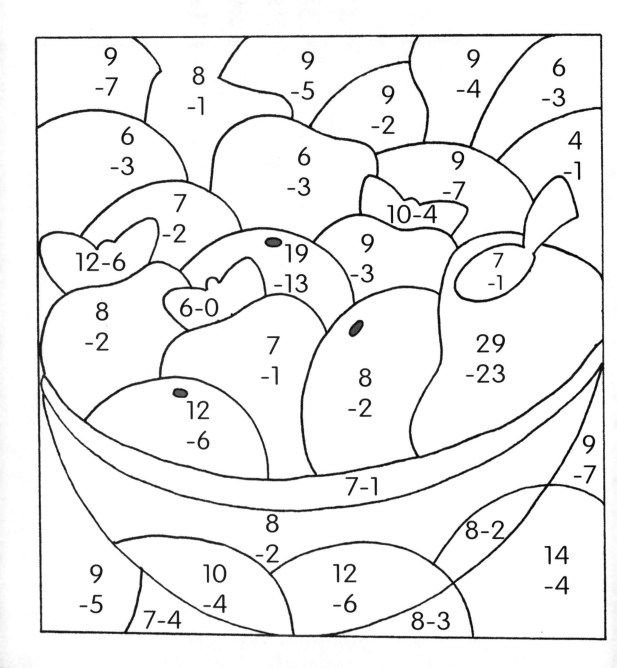

# Birthday Cake

Subtract the numbers. Write the answers on the balloons.

1.
$$\begin{array}{r} 11 \\ -\ 7 \\ \hline \end{array}$$
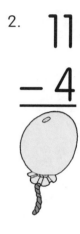

2.
$$\begin{array}{r} 11 \\ -\ 4 \\ \hline \end{array}$$

3.
$$\begin{array}{r} 10 \\ -\ 5 \\ \hline \end{array}$$

4.
$$\begin{array}{r} 11 \\ -\ 9 \\ \hline \end{array}$$

5.
$$\begin{array}{r} 12 \\ -\ 3 \\ \hline \end{array}$$

6.
$$\begin{array}{r} 13 \\ -\ 5 \\ \hline \end{array}$$

7.
$$\begin{array}{r} 12 \\ -\ 6 \\ \hline \end{array}$$

8.
$$\begin{array}{r} 11 \\ -\ 5 \\ \hline \end{array}$$

# Breakfast Buddies

Subtract the numbers.

1.
$$11$$
$$-\ 3$$

2.
$$12$$
$$-\ 5$$

3.
$$10$$
$$-\ 8$$

4.
$$11$$
$$-\ 5$$

5.
$$12$$
$$-\ 3$$

6.
$$11$$
$$-\ 8$$

7.
$$10$$
$$-\ 5$$

8.
$$12$$
$$-\ 7$$

# Tasty Tacos

Subtract the numbers.

1.  10
    − 6
    ___

2.  13
    − 7
    ___

3.  12
    − 9
    ___

4.  11
    − 2
    ___

5.  13
    − 5
    ___

6.  12
    − 8
    ___

7.  11
    − 6
    ___

8.  13
    − 8
    ___

# Hot Dogs and Hamburgers

Subtract the numbers.

1.  10
   − 9
   _____

2.  15
   − 6
   _____

3.  12
   − 6
   _____

4.  14
   − 7
   _____

5.  12
   − 4
   _____

6.  11
   − 4
   _____

7.  15
   − 7
   _____

8.  14
   − 9
   _____

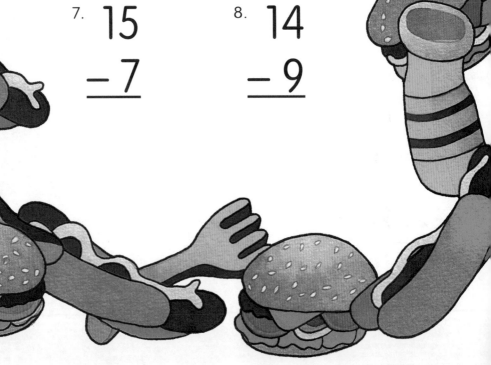

# Colorful Cotton Candy

Subtract the numbers.

1.
$$14 - 8$$

2.
$$16 - 9$$

3.
$$13 - 9$$

4.
$$11 - 2$$

5.
$$15 - 5$$

6.
$$13 - 5$$

7.
$$15 - 8$$

8.
$$14 - 6$$

# Eating Eggs for Breakfast

Write the answers on the lines.

Grandma made eggs for breakfast.

1. If she had 15 eggs and cooked 6 of them,

   how many eggs did she have left? _____

2. If she had 11 eggs and cooked 7 of them,

   how many eggs did she have left? _____

3. If she had 13 eggs and cooked 4 of them,

   how many eggs did she have left? _____

# Candy Clown

Subtract the numbers.

1. 12
   − 3

2. 14
   − 7

3. 18
   − 9

4. 15
   − 8

5. 14
   − 6

6. 11
   − 7

7. 12
   − 6

8. 15
   − 8

# Very Good Veggie

Subtract the numbers. Write the answers on the lines.

Color the picture for some extra fun.

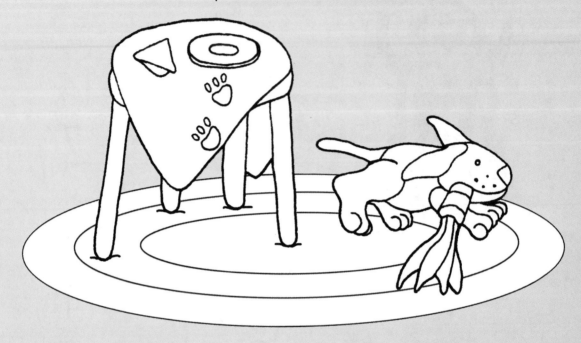

1. 11 − 3 = ___

2. 12 − 5 = ___

3. 18 − 9 = ___

4. 13 − 5 = ___

5. 12 − 5 = ___

6. 17 − 9 = ___

7. 13 − 7 = ___

8. 11 − 7 = ___

# A Cupcake Party

Fill in the blanks. Color the picture for some extra fun.

1. 12 – ___ = 8

2. 13 – ___ = 9

3. 11 – ___ = 3

4. 14 – ___ = 8

5. 17 – ___ = 9

6. 13 – ___ = 8

7. 18 – ___ = 9

8. 11 – ___ = 3

# Afternoon Snack

Subtract the numbers.

Color the areas that have the number 7 for the answer.

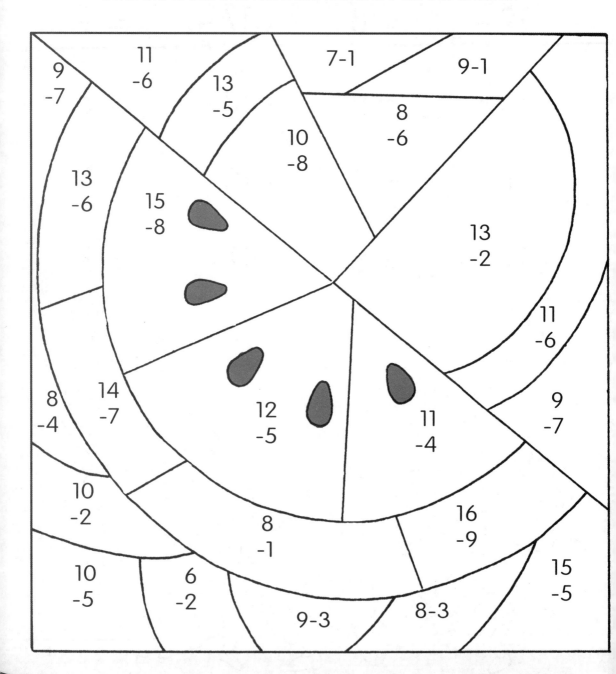

# Candy Cane Fun!

Subtract the numbers.

1.  17
    − 8
    ____

2.  14
    − 5
    ____

3.  16
    − 9
    ____

4.  14
    − 7
    ____

5.  12
    − 3
    ____

6.  11
    − 6
    ____

7.  10
    − 7
    ____

8.  14
    − 8
    ____

# Answer Key

**Page 4**
1. 3
2. 3
3. 1
4. 0
5. 3
6. 1
7. 1
8. 2

**Page 5**
1. 0
2. 3
3. 1
4. 1
5. 2
6. 2
7. 1
8. 1

**Page 6**
1. 2
2. 3
3. 3

**Page 7**
1. 1
2. 2
3. 5

**Page 8**
1. 4
2. 4
3. 3
4. 1
5. 0
6. 2
7. 2
8. 0

**Page 9**
1. 5
2. 1
3. 3
4. 4
5. 3
6. 1
7. 2
8. 4

**Page 10**

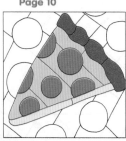

**Page 11**
1. 3
2. 2
3. 1
4. 4
5. 2

**Page 12**
1. 4
2. 1
3. 1
4. 2

**Page 13**
1. 1
2. 0
3. 1
4. 5
5. 1
6. 4
7. 3
8. 1

**Page 14**
1. 2
2. 3
3. 0

**Page 15**
1. 0
2. 2
3. 2

**Page 16**
1. 1
2. 4
3. 0
4. 2
5. 1
6. 6
7. 2
8. 5

**Page 17**
1. 4
2. 2
3. 1
4. 5
5. 3
6. 4
7. 2
8. 1

**Page 18**
1. 0
2. 3
3. 1
4. 2
5. 2
6. 6
7. 4
8. 3

**Page 19**
1. 2
2. 0
3. 3
4. 1
5. 1
6. 3
7. 0
8. 3

**Page 20**

**Page 21**
1. 4
2. 1
3. 3

**Page 22**
1. 4
2. 1
3. 2
4. 4
5. 5
6. 5

**Page 23**
1. 4
2. 1
3. 2

**Page 24**
1. 2
2. 3
3. 1

**Page 25**
1. 4
2. 1
3. 3

**Page 26**
1. 2
2. 5
3. 2
4. 4
5. 2
6. 4
7. 7
8. 1

**Page 27**
1. 0
2. 4
3. 1
4. 4
5. 1
6. 0
7. 6
8. 2

**Page 28**
1. 1
2. 6
3. 0
4. 4
5. 1
6. 3
7. 5
8. 5

**Page 29**
1. 0
2. 1
3. 5
4. 4
5. 1
6. 7
7. 2
8. 4

**Page 30**

**Page 31**
1. 2
2. 0
3. 2
4. 1
5. 5
6. 2
7. 1
8. 6

**Page 32**
1. 3
2. 1
3. 8
4. 0
5. 3
6. 3
7. 2
8. 7

**Page 33**
1. 2
2. 4
3. 5
4. 3
5. 5
6. 1
7. 2
8. 1

**Page 34**
1. 10
2. 40
3. 30
4. 20
5. ⑦⓪
6. 10
7. 40
8. 30

**Page 35**
1. 30
2. 10
3. 0
4. 40
5. 50
6. 30
7. 10
8. ⑥⓪

**Page 36**
1. 31
2. 44
3. 22
4. 41
5. 11
6. 23
7. 27
8. 22

**Page 37**
1. 21
2. 33
3. 24
4. 40
5. 24
6. 33
7. 23
8. 24

**Page 38**
1. 10
2. 22
3. 10
4. 24
5. 11
6. 12
7. 32
8. 33

## Answer Key

**Page 39**
1. 22
2. 13
3. 20
4. 4
5. 46
6. 12
7. 21
8. 35

**Page 40**

**Page 41**
1. 12
2. 11
3. 32
4. 11
5. 25
6. 45
7. 50
8. 22

**Page 42**
1. 33
2. 21
3. 53
4. 40
5. 27
6. 22
7. 11
8. 43

**Page 43**
1. 47
2. 72
3. 4
4. 30
5. 63
6. 35
7. 21
8. 44

**Page 44**
1. 13
2. 33
3. 21
4. 33
5. 11
6. 46
7. 21
8. 15

**Page 45**
1. 24
2. 11
3. 45
4. 32
5. 21
6. 31
7. 13
8. 21

**Page 46**
1. 31
2. 13
3. 42
4. 26
5. 31
6. 3
7. 22
8. 12

**Page 47**
1. 21
2. 25
3. 36
4. 62
5. 30
6. 52
7. 14
8. 34

**Page 48**
1. 41
2. 31
3. 34
4. 40
5. 2
6. 61
7. 41
8. 37

**Page 49**
1. 23
2. 24
3. 51

**Page 50**

**Page 51**
1. 4
2. 7
3. 5
4. 2
5. 9
6. 8
7. 6
8. 6

**Page 52**
1. 8
2. 7
3. 2
4. 6
5. 9
6. 3
7. 5
8. 5

**Page 53**
1. 4
2. 6
3. 3
4. 9
5. 8
6. 4
7. 5
8. 5

**Page 54**
1. 1
2. 9
3. 6
4. 7
5. 8
6. 7
7. 8
8. 5

**Page 55**
1. 6
2. 7
3. 4
4. 9
5. 10
6. 8
7. 7
8. 8

**Page 56**
1. 9
2. 4
3. 9

**Page 57**
1. 9
2. 7
3. 9
4. 7
5. 8
6. 4
7. 6
8. 7

**Page 58**
1. 8
2. 7
3. 9
4. 8

5. 7
6. 8
7. 6
8. 4

**Page 59**
1. 4
2. 4
3. 8
4. 6
5. 8
6. 5
7. 9
8. 8

**Page 60**

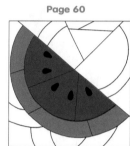

**Page 61**
1. 9
2. 9
3. 7
4. 7
5. 9
6. 5
7. 3
8. 6

# Congratulations,

_____
(Name)

You did a great job learning to subtract. Keep practicing your subtraction to get even better!

AWESOME!

Great Job!